OLIVIA RODRIGO

Making a Difference as a Pop Star

By Katie Kawa

I0807274

People Who Make a Difference

KidHaven PUBLISHING

Published in 2026 by
KidHaven Publishing, an Imprint of Greenhaven Publishing, LLC
2544 Clinton St.
Buffalo, NY 14224

Copyright © 2026 KidHaven Publishing, an Imprint of Greenhaven Publishing, LLC.

All rights reserved. No part of this book may be reproduced in any form without permission in writing from the publisher, except by a reviewer.

Designer: Deanna Lepovich
Editor: Katie Kawa

Photo credits: Cover, p. 19 Kathy Hutchins/Shutterstock.com; p. 5 Imagespace/Alamy Stock Photo; p. 7 WENN Rights Ltd/Alamy Stock Photo; p. 9 Geisler-Fotopress GmbH/Alamy Stock Photo; p. 11 JEP Live Music/Alamy Stock Photo; p. 13 UPI/Alamy Stock Photo; p. 15 Imago/Alamy Stock Photo; p. 17 DFree/Shutterstock.com; p. 21 (inset) Fred Duval/Shutterstock.com; p. 21 (background) T.Sumaetho/Shutterstock.com.

Library of Congress Cataloging-in-Publication Data

Names: Kawa, Katie, author.
Title: Olivia Rodrigo : making a difference as a pop star / Katie Kawa.
Description: [1.] | Buffalo, New York : KidHaven Publishing, 2026. | Series: People who make a difference | Includes index.
Identifiers: LCCN 2025011902 | ISBN 9781534549654 (library binding) | ISBN 9781534549647 (paperback) | ISBN 9781534549661 (ebook)
Subjects: LCSH: Rodrigo, Olivia–Juvenile literature. | Singers–United States–Biography–Juvenile literature. | Actors–United States–Biography–Juvenile literature. | LCGFT: Biographies.
Classification: LCC ML3930.R634 K39 2026 | DDC 782.42164092 [B]–dc23/eng/20250326
LC record available at https://lccn.loc.gov/2025011902

Printed in the United States of America

Some of the images in this book illustrate individuals who are models. The depictions do not imply actual situations or events.

CPSIA compliance information: Batch #CSKH26: For further information contact Greenhaven Publishing LLC at 1-844-317-7404.

Please visit our website, www.greenhavenpublishing.com. For a free color catalog of all our high-quality books, call toll free 1-844-317-7404 or fax 1-844-317-7405.

Find us on

CONTENTS

A Voice for Young Women	4
A California Girl	6
A Young Star	8
Suddenly a Superstar	10
Grammy Winner	12
She's Got *GUTS*	14
Raising Awareness	16
Fund 4 Good	18
It's Cool to Care	20
Glossary	22
For More Information	23
Index	24

A VOICE FOR YOUNG WOMEN

Pop music is often seen as a genre, or kind, of music that is popular with young women. This is certainly true for the music Olivia Rodrigo makes. As a young woman herself, she writes songs that other young women can **relate** to. This helps them feel less alone and like someone understands their big feelings.

Olivia is proud to be a voice for young women, and she's using her voice to call attention to issues young women care about. Through her music and her **activism**, she's become a voice for her **generation**, and she has no plans to quiet down.

In Her Words

"It's what I've gravitated [been drawn] towards my whole life — music that helps you process what you're feeling or comforts you when you're feeling these big feelings. It's just nice to know that someone else is experiencing [having] them. It makes you feel less alone."

— Interview with *Variety* magazine from November 2023

Olivia's music is popular with all kinds of people—not only young women. However, she's said she feels a special **responsibility** to take care of her female fans by loudly and proudly supporting causes that matter to them.

A CALIFORNIA GIRL

Olivia grew up near Los Angeles, California, but she didn't come from a Hollywood family. She was born on February 20, 2003, to parents with jobs far from show business. Her father was a **therapist**, and her mother was a teacher.

Olivia's parents knew their daughter was talented. Olivia is partly deaf in her left ear, but that didn't stop her from loving music. She started singing, dancing, and acting at a young age. In 2015, she starred in her first movie, *Grace Stirs Up Success*. It was a small movie, but big things were coming for Olivia.

In Her Words

"I would ... make up songs about being lost in the grocery store ... I was always singing."

— Interview with *Vogue* magazine from July 2023

Olivia's dad can trace some of his roots back to the Philippines. Olivia is proud of her Filipino heritage, or background.

A YOUNG STAR

In 2016, Olivia began acting in the Disney Channel TV show *Bizaardvark*. She played Paige Olvera, who was one of the show's main characters. On the show, Olivia played the guitar and sang. This gave the show's young viewers a look at Olivia's talent as a musician.

Bizaardvark ended in 2019, but Olivia wasn't done with Disney. That year, she took a starring role, or part, as Nini Salazar-Roberts in the Disney+ show *High School Musical: The Musical: The Series*. Olivia wrote the song "All I Want" for the show, and it became a hit, especially on **social media platforms** such as TikTok.

In Her Words

"You don't realize how young you are when you're young."

— Interview with *Vogue* magazine from July 2023

Olivia plays the guitar and the piano. She began writing her own songs at a young age, but "All I Want" was her first real taste of success as a songwriter.

SUDDENLY A SUPERSTAR

Olivia's star was on the rise, but it took one special song to make her a superstar. That song was "drivers license." After it came out in 2021, it quickly became the most popular song in the United States. People around the world also discovered it, thanks to its popularity on social media. The song told a story about young heartbreak that many people—from teenage girls to their dads—found relatable.

Later that year, Oliva came out with her first album, *SOUR*. It featured songs such as "drivers license" and "good 4 u," which also became a hit.

Even after *SOUR* came out, Olivia continued to be a part of *High School Musical: The Musical: The Series*. She ended her time with the show in 2022.

In Her Words

"I think that's why music is so magical. You can write about an experience [event] that you feel is really **unique** to you—and then you put it out and people from all different walks of life are like, 'I can really relate to this.'"

— Interview with the BBC from September 2023

GRAMMY WINNER

It takes a lot of hard work to make a hit album. The Disney+ **documentary** *Olivia Rodrigo: Driving Home 2 U* showed the work Olivia put into making *SOUR*. This documentary came out in 2022, which was a very big year for Olivia.

Not long after the documentary came out, Olivia won three Grammy Awards, which are the biggest honors in the music business. She won the award for Best Pop Solo Performance for "drivers license," as well as Best Pop Vocal Album for *SOUR*. She was also named Best New Artist, which is one of the most famous awards given out at the Grammys.

In Her Words

"I love writing about ... **vulnerable** things. It's my favorite thing to do, and I've never had a hard time doing it, because no one ever made me feel ashamed [bad] for showing my feelings."

— Interview with *The Face* magazine from November 2023

Olivia is shown here at the 2022 Grammy Awards, which were a major moment in her life as a musician.

SHE'S GOT *GUTS*

Olivia soon got to work on her second album. In 2023, *GUTS* came out, and it went right to the top of the Billboard 200 chart, which ranks the most popular albums in the United States. Songs such as "vampire" continued what Olivia had started with *SOUR*: They gave women an example of anger, which is something many women are taught to hide.

Another song on *GUTS* is "pretty isn't pretty," which is about how hard it can be for young women to like how they look. It helped Olivia's fans feel less alone in their struggles with **body image**.

In Her Words

"I could change up my body and change up my face
I could try every lipstick in every shade
But I'd always feel the same
'Cause pretty isn't pretty enough anyway"

— "pretty isn't pretty"

In 2024, Olivia's concert movie, *GUTS World Tour*, came out on Netflix. Through her music and her concerts, Olivia has shown her fans that it's OK to feel things such as sadness and anger and to express, or show, them. She believes this is an important thing for young women to learn, because it allows them to speak up when they're not being respected.

RAISING AWARENESS

Big feelings are at the heart of Olivia's music. She's also learned how to turn her big feelings into action when it comes to causes she cares about. She's worked with the Geena Davis Institute, which was started by actress Geena Davis to fight for better **representation** of women in movies and TV shows. Olivia has also raised money for groups that help women and girls around the world.

In addition, Olivia has helped raise money for people who are sick with certain skin diseases. She also raised awareness of ways to stay safe and healthy during the **COVID-19 pandemic**.

In Her Words

"So much of my fanbase is young girls and women, and so I think I feel a ... responsibility towards them to make them feel seen and heard and protected [safe], whether that's in the songs that I write or in the charities that I support."

— Interview with *Teen Vogue* magazine from October 2024

Olivia knows that her voice is powerful, so she's using it to call attention to issues in the world around her, especially issues related to equality and rights for women and girls.

FUND 4 GOOD

As Olivia was getting ready to go on tour in 2023, she decided she wanted to do even more to help women and girls around the world. She then started Fund 4 Good, which works to support groups that are fighting to make the world fairer and safer for women and girls.

When Olivia went on tour for the *GUTS* album, some of the money made through ticket sales went to Fund 4 Good and groups it supports in different countries. Some of these groups work to protect women from violence, or harm, and help women get health care.

In Her Words

"I think women are praised for always being nice and kind and helpful. And that's something that I've had to sort of outgrow as I grew up as a young woman in the world—that notion [ideal] of being sweet is the end-all ... There's a lot more ... to me than sweet."

— Interview with *GQ* magazine from August 2021

The Life of Olivia Rodrigo

2003
Olivia Rodrigo is born on February 20 in California.

2015
Olivia gets her first starring role in the movie *Grace Stirs Up Success*.

2016-2019
Olivia plays Paige Olvera in the TV show *Bizaardvark*.

2019
Olivia begins playing Nini Salazar-Roberts on *High School Musical: The Musical: The Series*.

2021
Olivia comes out with her first album, *SOUR*, which includes her hit song "drivers license."

2022
Olivia Rodrigo: Driving Home 2 U comes out on Disney+, Olivia wins 3 Grammy Awards, and she ends her time on *High School Musical: The Musical: The Series*.

2023
Olivia's second album, *GUTS*, comes out, and she starts Fund 4 Good.

2024
The concert movie *GUTS World Tour* comes out on Netflix.

2025
Olivia is chosen to headline the Glastonbury music festival.

Olivia may be young, but she has worked very hard to find success in the music business.

IT'S COOL TO CARE

In 2025, Olivia was chosen to be one of the headliners, or stars, of the Glastonbury music festival. This is a huge group of concerts held in England almost every year. Being chosen as a headliner is a huge honor, and it shows just how famous Olivia has become.

Olivia's music matters because it's driven by strong feelings, which reminds her fans that it's good to be open and honest about how you feel. Olivia Rodrigo isn't afraid to say that she cares—whether it's through her music or her support for causes that matter to her. She shows people that it's cool to care!

In Her Words

"We're so much more alike than we are different. At the core of it all, we're all feeling the same feelings of fear and sadness and loneliness and happiness and love."

— Interview with *Teen Vogue* magazine from October 2021

Be Like Olivia Rodrigo!

Raise money for groups that help women and girls. You could have a concert at your school to raise money!

Talk openly about the things you care about, and listen respectfully when others do the same. This reminds people that it's cool to care!

Support your friends and family members when they talk about their feelings, and never tease someone for sharing how they feel.

Find healthy ways to express big feelings. This could be writing a song about them, dancing them out, singing loudly to a song you can relate to, or talking to a friend or trusted adult about them.

Learn more about issues women and girls are dealing with around the world.

If someone you know is feeling sad or angry, write them something to help them feel less alone. This could be a letter, a card, or even a song.

Olivia Rodrigo has turned her big feelings into successful songs and important charity work, or work done to help others. These are some ways you can use your big feelings to make a difference like Olivia!

GLOSSARY

activism: Acting strongly in support of or against an issue.
body image: The way a person sees themselves and feels about how they look.
COVID-19 pandemic: An event that began in China in 2019 in which a disease that causes breathing problems, a fever, and other health issues spread rapidly around the world and made millions of people sick in a short period of time.
documentary: A nonfiction movie or television program presenting facts about a topic.
generation: A group of people born and living during the same time.
relate: To connect, understand, or respond, especially in a favorable way.
representation: The act of showing a group in a movie, a TV show, or another kind of media.
responsibility: A duty that a person should do.
social media platform: A website or application—also known as an app—that allows users to interact with each other and create online communities.
therapist: A person who is trained to help people understand and express their thoughts and feelings in a healthy way.
unique: Special or different from anything else.
vulnerable: Open about being hurt.

FOR MORE INFORMATION

WEBSITES

Billboard: Olivia Rodrigo

www.billboard.com/artist/olivia-rodrigo/

Billboard magazine's official website offers visitors a look at Olivia's life, a collection of videos and news stories about her, and a list of where her songs and albums have ended up on its charts.

Grammy Awards: Olivia Rodrigo

www.grammy.com/artists/Olivia-Rodrigo/38411

The official website of the Grammy Awards features facts about Olivia's life, lists of awards she's won, and news stories about her.

BOOKS

Andrews, Elizabeth. *Olivia Rodrigo: Best-Selling Songwriter*. Minneapolis, MN: DiscoverRoo, 2024.

Nguyen, Suzane. *Olivia Rodrigo*. Minneapolis, MN: Bellwether Media, 2025.

Rose, Rachel. *Olivia Rodrigo: Actress and Singer*. Minneapolis, MN: Bearport Publishing Company, 2023.

Publisher's note to educators and parents: Our editors have carefully reviewed these websites to ensure that they are suitable for students. Many websites change frequently, however, and we cannot guarantee that a site's future contents will continue to meet our high standards of quality and educational value. Be advised that students should be closely supervised whenever they access the internet.

INDEX

B

Bizaardvark (TV show), 8, 19
body image, 14

C

concerts, 14, 20, 21
COVID-19 pandemic, 16

D

Davis, Geena, 16
Disney+, 8, 12, 19
documentary, 12, 19

F

fans, 5, 14, 15, 16, 20
Filipino heritage, 7
Fund 4 Good, 18, 19

G

Grace Stirs Up Success (movie), 6, 19
Grammy Awards, 12, 13, 19
guitar, 8, 9
GUTS (album), 14, 18, 19

H

High School Musical: The Musical: The Series (TV show), 8, 11, 19

P

parents, 6, 7
piano, 9

S

songs, 4, 6, 8, 9, 10, 14, 16, 19, 21
SOUR (album), 10, 11, 12, 14, 19